1

INCOME INEQUALITY AND POVERTY
the impact on health and social care
Chris J Perry MA CSW
INDEX

Chapter	page
1 Introduction	3
2 Health and Social Care	8
3 Social Work	21
4 Children's Services and Youth Justice	28
5 Services for people with a disability, long term illness or mental health issue	41
6 Carers	49
7 A multi-disciplinary / inter-agency approach	53
8 Poverty, Health and Pensions	56
9 Economic Growth, income inequality and pensions	63
10 Housing	69
11 Salaries of the Super Rich and Utilities	77
12 The human and financial advantages of a whole systems approach	82

Income Inequality and Poverty – the impact on health and social care

2

"the love of money is the root of all evil"
The Apostle Paul

This is a special edition with enhanced biographical details for close family and friends which is available for all to buy.

Income Inequality and Poverty – the impact on health and social care

CHAPTER ONE – INTRODUCTION

This is effectively the second edition of my book "A Fair Society" re-titled in-order to keep the historical context of the first edition.

Rising income inequality and increasing poverty are the great social evils of our time. And unless Government does something to reverse the trend, given the correlation between income and demand upon the health services, the NHS will not keep pace with demand. Government will always be playing catch up.

"Trickle Down" economics and the privatisation of public services which has gathered momentum since the 1980's had, by the spring of 2025, created dozens of millionaires and turned millionaires into billionaires whilst the vast majority were little better off than they were before the 2008 Banking Crisis, whilst many more had fallen into poverty. Public services, especially the NHS, social care and housing had been eroded by policy decisions which had prioritised economic return over human need. And unless Government tackles pay differentials within companies, chasing inward investment in search of growth will make the rich richer and create low paid jobs for the masses as it has done since the 1980s.

Income Inequality and Poverty – the impact on health and social care

In April 2024 there were 4.5m children being brought up in poverty. 70% of whom had a parent in work. That was an increase of 0.2m over 2022/23. In March 2023 there were 107,317 children in the care of the local authority in the UK – the highest number ever. In December 2023, 112,660 homeless households were living in temporary accommodation in England, including 145,800 children. This was a record-high for both categories. Despite low detection rates the courts could not keep pace with demand and prisons were bursting at the seams. There was concern about rising knife crime amongst young people.

Two million older retired people were living in poverty in the UK in 2024. And despite the "triple lock" the state pension had fallen further behind earnings (23% in 2025 from 24.5% in 2020). What had widened the gap was the suspension of the "triple lock" in 2022 /23. Had the "triple lock" been applied the State Pension would have gone up by 8%, in line with the disputed figure for earnings which was thought to be a blip due to people returning to work after the pandemic, and the State Pension was only increased by 3.1%. Added to which stopping the "winter fuel allowance" in 2024 represented a further cut of 3% in the income associated with the universal state pension having been part of older retired people's income since 1999. Although it was restored for some, the following year, this was more out of concern for the opinion polls than for older people on the increased winter pressures on the NHS. Retired people got no benefit from the two pre-election cuts in National Insurance but did have to pay more income tax due to the freezing of the tax-free personal allowance and lost their free TV licence in 2022. Therefore, regrettably, after ten years of catching-up due to the "triple lock" which was introduced in 2010 to reverse the year-on-year erosion which had taken place since the earnings link was replaced with a prices link in the 1980's, older people were again being left behind reducing their quality of life and putting greater strain on the NHS and social care.

Widening income inequality and increasing poverty is a global issue. And in the Spring of 2025 Oxfam published its report "Takers Not Makers" which suggested that global billionaire wealth had increased by £1.5 trillion in 2024, a significant jump compared to the previous year. This increase translated to roughly £4.25 billion per day and was three times faster than the previous year. The total wealth of billionaires stood at £11.2 trillion. The number of billionaires also increased from 2,565 in 2023 to 2,769 in 2024. That was 204 more.

In contrast, according to the Office of National Statistics (ONS), the median household disposable income in the UK for the financial year ending 2023 was £34,500. This figure represents the middle-income level, with half of all households earning less than this amount and half earning more. This was a 2.5% decrease from the financial year ending 2022 when median income was £35,100. And according to research at Loughborough University for Marie Curie, approximately 111,000 people died in poverty in the UK in 2023, which was more than 300 people per day. This number represented a 19% increase compared to the 93,000 deaths in poverty reported in 2019.

Morris Pearl, Chair of the Patriotic Millionaires and a former Managing Director at BlackRock said: "Rising and extreme inequality threatens everything we hold dear: our democracies, our planet, and our broader society...." And the Resolution Foundation anticipated that if the economic forecasts and policies remained unchanged, an additional 1.5 million people, including 400,000 children, would be in relative poverty in the UK after housing costs by 2029/30.

Although, widening income inequality and increasing poverty is a global issue and one which must be tackled internationally. This book is intended to be a catalyst to debate and considers those issues and possible solutions which would be within the gift of the UK Government: particularly in respect of health, social care, housing, criminal justice, children, the utilities and pensions.

It will take "Political Will" driven by "popular demand" to bring about change. The challenge is to get, and keep, people talking about the issues and possible solutions so that they become familiar and thereby acceptable and begin to gain traction.

Perhaps the government should do an inequality and poverty audit on all it does to ensure it is reducing income inequality and poverty and not increasing them?

CHAPTER TWO
HEALTH AND SOCIAL CARE.

Lord Darzi's 2024 review of the NHS confirmed it was in crisis. Although Lord Darzi stopped short of recommending the radical reform, restructuring and cultural change, based on a whole systems review the NHS required, he did refer to the social determinates of health, and in particular poverty and poor housing, which were increasing the demand upon the NHS.

Lord Darzi's review was twenty-eight years after the then Government set up the "Royal Commission on Long Term Care" and four years after the Health and Social Care Act 2021 which it was claimed would:

> i. sort out the under-funding of social care;
> ii. remove the need for people to sell their houses to pay for their care;
> iii. promote joined-up service delivery;
> iv. replace the competitive model with a collaborative one.

Four years after the 2021 Act, and the injection of £57.5b, the crisis in Social Care had deepened. So much so that the Government asked Dame Louise Casey to carry out a review with an interim report in

Income Inequality and Poverty – the impact on health and social care

2026 and a final report in 2028. The Government continued to push ahead with its revitalisation of the NHS, (with the abolition of NHS England) and with Local Government Reform: despite there being widespread agreement that one cannot resolve the problems of the NHS without sorting out the crisis in social care.

Social Care is a Local Government Responsibility and the NHS a central Government one which after the abolition of NHS England has been managed directly by The Department of Health and Social Care.

It is vital that people do not stay in hospital longer than they need for their own sakes, to avoid deterioration, and to free up hospital beds. A survey by "The Times" newspaper in 2025 estimated there were on average 13,600 older people every day in hospital who did not need to be awaiting social care.

A general hospital ward bed was estimated to cost around £586 per day in 2025. Therefore, this was costing the NHS £2.9m per year. No doubt there will be Financial Directors in the NHS who would argue that this would be a opportunity, rather than a real saving, as the cost would still be there. However, if the NHS needs more hospital beds there would be a saving in not having to build them at an additional capital cost in addition to the revenue cost.

Income Inequality and Poverty – the impact on health and social care

The average cost of home care in 2025 was estimated at £250 per day compared with £586 for a hospital bed. Therefore, to sort this out would clearly save money a minimum of £1.5m per year. This would either require an investment in social care or reduced demand as there are probably more people being supported in the community than are waiting discharge who, if their social care was withdrawn, would end up in hospital. This has always been a balancing act for Social Service Departments and not always fully understood by health professionals working in the hospitals.

It is vital that patients are not discharged to care homes against their wishes, as they appear to have been during the COVID 19 pandemic, as this is one of the few irreversible decisions in life. Once one has given up one's home it is very difficult in later life to start over. All people entering care homes should be able to fully discuss the implications, both financial and emotional, with a social worker before agreeing to enter a care home and be able to retain their house for at least six months before taking a final decision as to their future – as legislation requires.

Radical reform, cultural change and re-structuring of the NHS and social care is required based on a whole systems approach. And, given the correlation between income and health, unless Government does something about the widening income inequality and increasing poverty in our society the NHS and social care will not keep pace with demand and will always be playing catch up.

The proposed cap at £86,000 on the amount which could have been spent on care home fees, in the 2021 Health and Social Care Act, was suspended by the incoming Labour Government in 2024. However, the cap would have favoured the rich in that people who did not have sufficient savings would still have had to sell their house to pay for their care. And the Act did not address the anomaly whereby someone with cancer gets free terminal care whereas for someone with Alzheimer's Disease or dementia their care is means tested. Looking after someone with Alzheimer's Disease or dementia is extremely stressful due to interrupted sleep, fear of wandering or leaving a gas tap on, not being recognised by someone one loves, and the guilt at letting them go into a care home.

The "Integrated Care Systems" and "Integrated Care Partnerships" introduced by the 2021 Act proved very costly, bureaucratic and cumbersome and appeared more concerned with:

> i. preserving the then configuration of local government and NHS Trusts, and;

ii.   protecting the purchaser / provider split and commissioning, to promote the mixed economy of care;

than the provision of integrated care. The mind set had not changed.

Change must be led by research into cause and effect.

Successive Governments have tried to get health, social services, police, education and housing to work together, from joint funding in the 1970s to the pooling of budgets and health and social care trusts. This has applied equally to child protection and adult social care. They have had the tools to tell them things are not working but have lacked the tools to put them right leading to repeated re-organisation. And none has grasped the nettle of different geographical areas, different funding streams and different lines of accountability, which have been the main impediments.

Although, the proposals for Local Government Re-organisation contained in the "English Devolution White Paper" published in December 2024 would bring housing (responsible for warden systems and homelessness) together with Social Services it does not include Health or the Police.

Income Inequality and Poverty – the impact on health and social care

There is just as much empirical evidence in respect of organisation, management and leadership as there is medicine, social policy and social work and yet this is rarely applied in practice. For many years, until the late 1980s, Brunel University received Department of Health funding to apply "organisational analysis" to health and social care including "the stratification of work and organisational design" (Billis and Rowbothan, 1985). The Tom Peters Group has studied cultural change, customer care, motivation and leadership (Peters, 1992). And applying his unique whole systems methodology to a hospital in Holland, Christian Schumacher (the son of the author of "Small Is Beautiful" and author of "God in Work") was able to achieve a 30% increase in output with higher morale and lower sickness levels (Bainton, 1995).

Social Service and Health Service Managers are extremely lucky in that the majority of their staff are working in their chosen vocation; it is what they want to do. It should therefore be possible to arrive at a situation whereby they can say, as many sports people do, aren't I lucky I am doing what I want to do and being paid for it. Why then was morale reportedly so low?

People in Health and Social Care are working in some very stressful situations but which can be very

14

rewarding if they see the outcome of their work and the improvement they have brought about in people's lives.

Unfortunately, many hospitals are still organised on the discredited production line model with, for example, some nurses just taking blood, not knowing why, the results or outcome for the patient.

During 2025 I had three spells in hospital. The NHS, ambulance crew, doctors and nurses saved my life and could not have been more caring. However, there were signs that they felt undervalued by their employer: not by their patients although some were very demanding. One of the signs of feeling undervalued is being precious about demarcation and not doing anything seen as beneath one. I was in a side room with an ensuite unable to get out of bed due to having both a catheter and drip. A nurse came to take my blood pressure and I asked if she would mind filling my water jug as I had been told to drink. The jug could have been filled in my room as there was a sink and tap in the corner as well as the ensuite. However, she said she would get somebody. She then went out of my room and I watched her disappear down the corridor which went straight from my door which had a large window. Three or four minutes later she returned and said someone was just coming. Two or three minutes later someone appeared in the distance coming down the corridor towards me. She came in confirmed I needed some water and filled the jug. A consequence of this strict adherence to demarcation was that it took two people a combined ten minutes to do a thirty second job.

The use of Agency Staff also distracts from the continuity of care. Agency Staff are very expensive, with money going on travel, lodgings and agency fees. It should not be beyond the wit of managers and trades unions to manage without them until there is no work and they have to apply for permanent positions and the savings shared in higher salaries for all permanent staff.

The changes of the last thirty years have added to the cost and fragmentation of services.

Prior to the creation of NHS Trusts and the demise of Area Health Authorities my counterpart in health managed nine hospitals, five of which were regional, community services and the Family Practitioners Committee (GPs) all with a management team smaller than is now found in every NHS Trust. Prior to the 1995 local government re-organisation, in Wales, health and social services had common geographical boundaries, with several joint All Wales Strategies, although housing was a District Council responsibility and Health and

Social Services did not have common funding streams or lines of accountability.

Wales went from 8 County Councils and 37 District Councils to 22 Unitary Authorities at colossal expense when had the County Councils been made the Unitary Authorities there would have been immediate savings on the cost of democracy and year on year savings as District Council Departments were merged and some with County Council Departments. And the coterminousity of boundary between health and social services would also have been preserved. A win win.

Similar, re-organisation in England and the splitting of Children's and Adult Social Services together with the re-location of other responsibilities also added to the cost and fragmentation.

At the time of writing, in the Spring of 2025, there were 24 County Councils, 181 District Councils, 58 Unitary Authorities, 36 Metropolitan Boroughs and 32 London Boroughs in England and 22 County Councils in Wales, 223 NHS Trusts and 43 Police Authorities. All serving different geographical areas, with different funding streams and different lines of accountability.

The Government estimated that the reform of Local Government contained in its "White Paper" published in

December 2024, which will effectively take out District Councils and redraw the boundaries of some unitary authorities, would save £2.9billion pounds. Parish or Community Councils remain. The NHS and Police were not included.

Shortly after taking up office in 2024 the Prime Minister said there would be no more funding for the NHS without reform. Therefore, the savings identified from Local Government Reform and the abolition of NHS England could be used to pump prime a ripple effect of whole systems reform.

To include Health and the Police by returning them to local democratic control would have improved efficiency and joint working with further savings. This would also have removed the need for the "integrated care systems" and save millions on the cost of democracy, and management, whilst making services more democratically accountable.

Smaller geographical areas, less responsibility and less directly managed provision.

In 1974 there were 120 Social Service Authorities – at the time of writing, in 2025, there were 172. Children's and Adult Services had been split into separate departments in England – increasing the number to

322. Many responsibilities, such as "Registration and Inspection", had been removed and placed elsewhere.

Long Term Care

Prior to 1980 the majority of care homes were provided by Local Authorities under Part III of the 1948 National Assistance Act. Margaret Thatcher extended choice by enabling people to have their fees in private and voluntary care homes paid by the then Benefits Agency subject only to the availability of a place and a means test. This led to a rapid growth in privately run "care homes" and the cost escalated to billions which Sir Roy Griffiths termed the "perverse incentive" (Griffiths, 1988) as the money was not available for home care and it was thought there were people in residential care who neither wanted nor needed to be. The money was transferred to Local Authority Social Service Departments, by the 1990 National Health Service and Community Care Act which had to carry out an "assessment of need" and "verification of wishes". What had been an "open-ended entitlement" became a "cash limited allocation" with Social Service Departments charged with "managing the market". The majority fixed their "contract price" below the cost of their in-house provision (so much for the level playing field) which hastened the demise of in-house provision and meant that private and voluntary homes struggled financially and had to subsidise local authority placements from the fees of private residents. At the time of the 2021 Health and Social Care Act 10% of independent care homes were in financial difficulty and under threat of closure. And during 2022, 191 care homes closed. Many of the larger chains with multiple care homes borrowed money on the open market, sometimes paying themselves bonuses, and added the cost of loan repayment to the weekly cost of the home.

The 1990 National Health Service and Community Care Act included the funding for Nursing Homes, which had previously been a Health Authority responsibility, so that for the first time they became means tested although the nursing element was subsequently disregarded.

The money transferred from the Benefits Agency was also available for home care. Prior to 1990 there were very few private domiciliary care agencies and those there were, were very expensive. Domiciliary Care Agencies grew like topsy and the imposition of the purchaser / provider split brought the prices down and with prices the wages.

This transfer from public to private sector provision continued under its own momentum, unchecked, for decades so that by 2025 there was very little public sector residential or domiciliary care for older people left. And even Children's Homes and Fostering Agencies were increasingly in the independent sector and not directly managed.

There were by 2025 probably very few people working in health and social care who remembered when most provision was directly managed and Local Authorities bought into specialist independent provision only if it would better meet the needs of their client and grant aided the voluntary sector.

CHAPTER THREE – SOCIAL WORK.

Even the nature of social work itself has changed – so much so that social work is grossly undervalued and social workers misused.

In the late 1960s and early 1970s social work was regarded as a valuable resource in its own right and social workers seen as "agents of change". Since then, social workers have been increasingly regarded as "gate keepers" assessing the eligibility for practical help and rationing of services.

The Seebohm Report (Seebohm, 1968) which led to the 1970 Social Services Act and the establishment of Social Service Departments in 1971 recognised the value of social work and saw social workers as the key resource. There was a wide debate at the time as to whether they should be called "social service departments" or "social work departments" as they were in Scotland. However, The Seebohm Report did not create the "one door to knock on", it promised, as a multi-disciplinary / inter-agency response is often required in differing combinations depending upon the desired outcome. This was subsequently recognised with the establishment of Area Child Protection Committees and Child Protection Procedures (post Maria Caldwell), Mental Health procedures, the creation of "Community Mental Handicap Teams" (now Learning Disability), and Youth Justice Teams etc.

Between the implementation of the 1970 Social Services Act and the 1974 Local Government Re-organisation, Social Service Departments flourished and benefitted from considerable growth.

The undoing of much of the public sector was down to the philosophy of the Thatcher years and more particularly, in respect of Health and Social Services, to Sir Roy Griffiths and, what was to me, his mistaken belief that people were motivated by and could be controlled by money. This led to the introduction of the contract culture and internal market with the purchaser / provider split which Sir Roy thought would create a level playing field to facilitate a mixed economy of care thereby forcing quality up and prices down. It has subsequently been proven to have had the opposite effect and led to over-prescription taking away the ability of carers to react in situ to changing need. It also led to greater fragmentation with different components of a "package of care" bought from different providers.

Unlike Freddie Seebohm, Sir Roy Griffiths appeared to have little understanding of the nature of social work. A consequence of which was that Social Workers were deployed on the "purchasing side", assessing the need for specific services (often responding to "presenting problems" rather than the "underlying problem") which led to several social services departments providing "minding" rather than "mending" services with an ever-increasing workload of dependent people.

Brought up in the days of Florence Hollis (Hollis, 1964), who described social work as a "psycho-social process", I have always considered social work to be about the use of relationship, and various therapeutic techniques, to bring about change. Social Workers need to begin where the client is (I personally dislike the term "user") and convey empathy with their client's perceived problem. Taking a social history, itself a form of catharsis, and identifying the underlying problems. Before:

i)   **Helping the client to reach his/her own decisions and resolve his/her own problems** by the social worker asking open ended questions, waiting and if necessarily repeating to enable the client time to think. Making a good use of thought-provoking silence.

ii) **Counselling and therapeutic help.** Other techniques used by social workers can help the client to come to terms with reality and consider the options, deal with ambivalence, improve motivation, relieve depression and improve inter-personal relationships.

iii) **Lowering or increasing anxiety to improve functioning** – this was key to my work as a social worker, manager and agent of change. Too high a level of anxiety or too low a level of anxiety will impede functioning. In the 1960s the NSPCC would usually increase the level of anxiety, through threat of consequence, believing it would improve functioning and the FSU (Family Service Units) take the opposite view and provide support to reduce the level of anxiety to increase functioning. Neither were able to measure where the level of anxiety was to start with. I would consider this at depth both when working with clients, supervising staff and managing organisations. Anxiety is an intrinsic part of culture and one needs to optimise the anxiety level, not too high and not too low, of an organisation for it to work both effectively and efficiently.

iv) **budgeting and negotiation with creditors**; asking the client (or clients) to write down and prioritise their expenditure against income. Look at ways of increasing income or reducing expenditure and prioritisation. Negotiating re-payment by instalment with creditors. As a social worker I always found that people were far more willing to pay instalments via me than direct to a rent collector for example.

v) **Involving friends and relatives in physical care** – gaining acceptance of the need for help, asking who might be able to help, permission to approach them and discuss difficulties, see response and what they might do, test this is genuine and not just as a result of the visit, do they really have the time and motivation etc. Agree who is to do what and when with all concerned.

vi) **changing external factors in the environment** etc etc. This can involve a whole range of things from "care proceedings" in respect of children, to the provision of aids, adaptations or rehousing. To negotiating with creditors, employers, the police or local authority. Or helping to find work or sheltered placement.

vii) **arranging practical help and support** – both voluntary and paid

Underpinning this work is a thorough knowledge of "human growth and behaviour", the importance of the first five years and Freudian Theory of the ID (animal instincts) Super Ego (developed conscience) and the Ego (arbitrator), the conscious, sub-conscious and unconscious, and the maturation process. Social Workers also have a grounding in psychology and sociology and an understanding of prejudice. Social Workers also make use of "transference", "transactional analysis" and use such techniques as "a systems approach to family therapy" etc etc

These are the "generic" (not to be confused with "generalist") skills of social workers. They then need the specialist knowledge of their areas of work whether it be working with people with specific disabilities or illnesses, mental illness, older people, youth justice, domestic abuse and marital counselling, parenting skills and child protection, fostering and adoption, registration and inspection, homelessness or work with adult offenders. And a detailed knowledge of the legislative framework in which they work, the law and resources available on which they can draw.

It is then important that social workers are engaged on the work which interests and motivates them as social work is a vocation. People may be attracted to a job by the salary but once in post people are motivated by job satisfaction and recognition of a job well done.

CHAPTER FOUR
CHILDREN'S SERVICES AND YOUTH JUSTICE.

In recent times it has concerned me that in child protection the emphasis appears to have been increasingly on "safeguarding" rather than understanding and bringing about lasting change. Doctors can indicate whether, or not, they consider an injury to be non-accidental, the police can bring a prosecution or temporarily remove the perpetrator, but it is for the social worker to determine what caused the incident, the likelihood of it recurring and if it might what, if anything, might be done to ensure that it doesn't. All too often case conferences are held to decide whether a child should be returned home when none of those present are able to say what they have done to bring about change in the situation, to warrant even consideration of a return home, and the discussion solely around the additional safeguarding measures required to reduce risk.

In March 2023 there were 107,317 children in the care of the local authority in the UK – the highest number ever. These children were mainly taken into care for abuse or neglect. And it is not uncommon for children taken into care for their own protection to exhibit understandably disturbed behaviour as a reaction to removal from home which if not dealt with can escalate and sometimes result in them being transferred to residential resources intended for children taken into care for disturbed behaviour or offending from where they emerge as offenders. Counselling by a social worker is key.

The Government appointed Josh MacAlister to undertake a review of children's services in 2021 and he reported in May 2022. Since then, greater emphasis on early intervention and preventing the need to receive children in to care has been encouraged.

During 2024 there were increasing concerns about knife crime amongst young people, unacceptable delays in the court system, prisons bursting at the seams and yet most reported crime went unresolved. It is detection, not punishment, which is the real deterrent and detection rates were very low and only bolstered by "taken into accounts".

In the more deprived areas of the UK in 2025 there is very little for teenagers to do, poor living conditions and little hope for the future. In consequence they are a breeding ground for gangs and delinquent behaviour. There are children and young people with very little hope or aspiration. How can we punish children for behaviour which is a direct result of the society into which they have been born?

I first became aware of the adverse effect of stigma and labelling during adolescence during my early teens when cycling to grammar school I would pass children who had failed the eleven plus walking to the secondary modern school. They clearly felt very inferior and in my late teens I became a strong advocate of Comprehensive Education.

Having helped with cubs from the age of 14, I was given special dispensation to be warranted as a cub master at 16 (normally 21) and had begun running scout and guide socials, from the age of 15. These also raised money for the scout group and later the Community Association. This was in the days of Teddy Boys and in the early days they would gather outside the Scout Hut, throw bricks on the roof and intimidate young people as they went to the outside toilet. Possibly as a result of teenage bravado but also in the knowledge I had scores of young people behind me, I went outside and invited them to come in. Much to my surprise they scarpered! One by one, over the next few weeks they came in. Initially, I would be asked to play record requests with a fist in my face – one such record was "beatnik fly"- which I was asked to play four or five times in one evening! However, as time went by and my productions got bigger, moved to larger premise and began managing "rock groups" these lads became my bouncers. Instead of anti-social behaviour they became the custodians of law and order. It was this experience which led to a change in career from aeronautical engineering, having been offered a place at Swansea University, to social work: although my first job was working with older people and homeless families many of whom had multiple problems.

So, what could social workers working with children, young people and families and in Youth Offending Teams do to improve the situation?

Many children, who offend, commit their first offence whilst truanting from school because they are already on the wrong side of the law and have been labelled as such. Children should want to go to school and not have to be made to do so. Social workers, and Young Offending Teams, already liaise with schools to look at what they might do differently to attract the non-attenders on their caseloads and this could be developed further.

Given what we know about adolescent behaviour it is hardly surprising that many young people go on offending sprees between apprehension for an offence and disposal through the courts which is why this period needs to be kept as short as possible and to a matter of days rather than weeks.

Most issues that social workers deal with require a multi-disciplinary / inter-agency approach and it is vital that all relevant parties, from practitioner to senior managers work together to reduce delay.

Group residential intervention, be it Young Offender Institutions or residential care (secure or otherwise), for young people has been shown to reinforce offending and establish a pattern of offending for life. As per the 1970s ITV documentary "Creating Criminals".

During my social work training in the early 1960s my residential placement was in a Remand Home. When boys arrived the others would gather around and ask what they had done. Which would usually be greeted by "Oh, is that all". The story would get progressively serious with each telling and the main topic of conversation was crime.

Even if children were rehabilitated the local community would, on their return home, expect them to behave as before and they would soon be forced back into role and revert to past behaviour.

There is therefore little wonder that re-offending rates are so high following residential intervention.

So, how should social workers deal with children who offend? The answer is to separate and occupy.

Children and young people who offend need to be fully occupied throughout their waking hours on activities which interest and motivate them, so they grow out of their offending.

Community-based activities are not cheap and have to be adequately resourced because of the risks involved. They are also very visible and, as such, can lead to criticism of rewarding bad behaviour. Society is happier to spend £130,000 per child per year on Young Offenders Institutions which is seen as punishment, even though it does not work, than a fraction of that cost on constructive intervention. I was once criticized in the Times Educational Supplement for allegedly rewarding bad behaviour. Two social workers were going on holiday and asked if they could take one of their girls with them. The girl was excluded from school and had never been on an aeroplane or out of the country. All they asked was permission and that the Local Authority pay for the girls holiday. They would look after her for free effectively working their holiday. The package holiday, and not having to pay the social workers, meant it was cheaper than her placement in South Glamorgan. She was excluded from school so even had she not gone on holiday she would not have been in school.

This, together with a week of the undivided attention of the two social workers, worked wonders. When she came back the social workers negotiated her re-admittance to school and she went as she no longer felt deprived or different and could join to conversations about foreign holidays and flying. She never looked back.

Therefore, all agencies employing members of the Young Offenders Team need to clearly state their intentions and stress that the approach is both cheaper and more effective and publicise the statistical outcomes.

In-order to overcome stigma and labelling it is important that some of the activity should involve face to face contact with people in need (such as the CSV Children in Care Programme of the1970s and 1980s) to change the perception from delinquent to helper in both the young person's own eyes and those of those around them.

Special activities run jointly with and involving the police can help the young person's perception of, and attitude toward, the police. There was a craze in Greater Manchester, when I worked in Bolton, of joy riders stealing cars and looking for police cars for the fun of a police car chase. And in South Glamorgan the police were involved in a project called "dragon wheels" helping youngster to learn how to repair and look after cars and drive around a track becoming aware of the dangers to themselves and others of not driving safely.

Involvement in organised sport and all kinds of structured recreational activity and hobbies should also be included.

Involving young people in environmental projects will give them ownership, so that instead of defacing them they will protect them. Children who regularly played football damaging flower beds were involved in the planting of those beds and without being asked made sure balls kept off their plants after that.

Restorative Justice whereby the young person is brought face to face with their victim(s) to discuss the consequences of their behaviour can also bring about lasting change,

The danger is that Courts use their powers to prescribe community activity which is then less effective as the value is in the young person wanting to take part voluntarily.

For those young people who are beyond parental control and cannot be supported at home professional (or paid) foster carers have been shown to be effective.

There is little point holding parents accountable for their children's behaviour during adolescence. Adolescence is a period of rapid physical and emotional change during which the young person is trying to establish an identity independent of their parents. It is a time of insecurity when peer group support is essential but can be detrimental due to "egging on" which is why parents often say their child has got into bad company – which is what all the parents of that group of children say. Therefore, there is little point putting pressure on parents who will already have a high anxiety level as that will only make things worse. Steps need to be taken to reassure parents and to reduce their anxiety level to improve functioning. They may be responsible for their child's behaviour but if they have not got a positive relationship with their child when (s)he reaches adolescence it is too late: they cannot go back a relive the early years.

The early years are the formulative ones when children learn right from wrong and form many of their values, prejudices, behaviours and motivations which will remain with them for life. There are now 3.9 million children being brought up in poverty – 2/3rds of whom have a parent in work. Children brought up in poverty are less likely to do well at school, more likely to have health problems, making a demand upon the NHS, and have a shorter life expectancy. These families need emotional and practical help and social workers need to take every opportunity through their professional associations to raise concern about the human and financial cost of widening income inequality and increasing poverty in our society. There is little point throwing more and more money at the first aid camp at the bottom of the cliff without building a fence at the top.

Although not cheap community-based intervention and policies of diversion and alternatives to custody are cheaper than counter-productive secure residential accommodation and therefore there is money available to re-deploy to early intervention and preventative work with families, particularly those with children under five, to reduce the number of children needing to be taken into care.

There is nothing new in what is advocated here and all within the gift of those working in the field. It does not require legislation or additional resources. It is over forty years since what became known as the "Bolton Child Care Package". (See "The Shocking Case of a Successful Department" - Social Work Today 19/5/81 and "Nothing Succeeds Like Success" - Community Care 1-10-81) The number of children in the care of Bolton Metropolitan Borough was reduced from 660 to 487, between 1975 and 1982 and those in residential care from 286 to 107. By 1982 there had been no children in Community Homes with Education (CHEs) or secure accommodation for over a year and the number of crimes associated with young people had fallen quite dramatically.

Similar policies of "diversion and alternatives to custody" were pursued in South Glamorgan County Council in the 1980s under the banner of "The Strategy to Reduce the Crime Rate". In both Bolton and South Glamorgan all targets in respect of both outcome and budget were met and money re-deployed into early intervention and preventative work with families, particularly those with children under five. In South Glamorgan a network of multi-disciplinary / inter-agency Family Centres were developed in which social workers and other professionals working with children and families and child protection in the nieghbourhood were based - the most recent of which were integral to schools. This enabled the provision of selective help to those in need within a universal framework of support to all to reduce stigma and labelling and include teachers within the multi-disciplinary team. There was also an integrated youth justice system, and Youth Court Bureau which worked hard to reduce delay, and an array of community-based activities and occupations. The number of offences associated with juveniles in South Glamorgan fell by 34.3% between 1983 and 1993 and by a further 8% in 1994. In 1983 there were 94 children placed out-County in high-cost Community Homes with Education on the premises: by 1995 there had been none for several years. Very little, if any, use was made of secure accommodation and there were no children in prison. Between 1983 and 1995 the number of children in care (legal status – including those "looked after" and home "charge and control") was reduced from 986 to 274 and those in residential care from 386 to 87.

One cannot resolve whole system problems with component level solutions. It is how resources are distributed and used which is the big issue.

Structural change in Society

In the 1940s, 50s and 60s it was unusual for both parents to work and school hours were from 8-45 am to 4-15 pm during which children were not allowed off the premises. Children either left school at 14, 15 or 16 and went into apprenticeships, where they had one to one supervision from an adult, or went into small sixth forms where the same school attendance rules applied and they were often given responsibility as prefects. Now it is the norm for both parents to work, of necessity (if they can), and schools turn out at 3 pm or earlier. Older children go to six form colleges, where they are grouped together (potentially encouraging anti-social behaviour – through "egging on) and not given responsibility for the younger children as prefects or confined to the campus and sometimes only have to college two or three days per week. It is a wonder there is not more anti-social behaviour and vandalism.

From the age of seven to eighteen I would cycle to school leave my bicycle in the cycle racks, unchained, and it would always be there at the end of the school day. Three friends and I would cycle to the travelling fairs at week-ends and leave our quite expensive bicycles which were the envy of many of our friends on the grass verge, unchained, and they would always be there to cycle home. In the 1960s I had new Zephyr 6s (Z car equivalent) There was a garage in Sheffield without parking. When I collected it after servicing, I would be told turn left out of here and you will find it on the left-hand side of the second or third street on the right and the key is in the ash tray! It was always there.

CHAPTER FIVE
SERVICES FOR PEOPLE WITH A DISABILITY, LONG-TERM ILLNESS OR MENTAL HEALTH ISSUE.

In February 2024 there were 6.9m people, or 10.4% of the working age population, claiming disability benefit. This included benefits like Personal Independence Payment (PIP) or Disability Living Allowance (DLA) and the Universal Credit Health Journey. The priority of the incoming Government was to get people off benefit and back into work. However, 51% of people with a permanent physical disability were in employment compared with only 4.8% of people with a learning disability.

The Government reinforced its intention to get as many people as possible with disabilities and health conditions into work in the April 2025 financial statement. It stated that it was trying to "reduce dependency" on benefits, which meant that the amount that many people with disabilities were entitled to for health-related or disability- related support could decrease. There was a revolt amongst Labour MPs and combined with the opposition benches forced the

Government to modify its intention to only include new claimants.

Any one of us could find ourselves with a physical disability or chronic sickness (physical or mental) often without warning or time to prepare. Clearly, we would need counselling and social work support and measures to reduce our anxiety and not threats to increase it through loss of benefit. Most people with permanent disabilities or chronic illness would love to be fit and able to work. However, if the Government believes a financial incentive is required it would be better to increase their earning potential rather than the threat of increased poverty.

It is very difficult for someone with a disability who has been off work for some time to go straight into work. They need a period of rehabilitation, re-climatising, training and getting used to getting up and out to work in the morning. This is where "transitional sheltered workshops" can help. Even better if they were enclaves in normal places of work, making the transfer to normal employment that much easier.

In the 1990's "Sheltered Placement" enabled employers to take people with a physical disability or learning disability on at the same rate of pay as its other employees and receive a subsidy to compensate for lower output subject to an assessment by the then Disablement Resettlement Officer. This was superseded by Universal Credit which included additional support for people with health conditions or disabilities which limited their ability to work. The department for Work and Pensions assessed this "capability to work" to determine eligibility for extra amounts based on individual circumstance. In addition to which the Access to Work scheme could provide grants to cover practical support such as equipment, adaptations or support workers needed to work. It could also include help with transportation, mental health support and communication support at job interviews. However, these all have to be applied for by the individual and give little incentive to the employer.

Since the 1970 Chronically Sick and Disabled Persons Act the emphasis has been on normalisation and huge strides have been made in making public buildings more accessible for people with mobility problems, with ramps, lifts and blue badges etc, although adaptations for people with visual and hearing impairment have not kept pace.

Thankfully the segregation of people with disabilities in Sheltered Workshops, those for blind people often involving dipping bristles in boiling pitch to make brushes which would hardly pass the health and safety regulations today, and people with learning disabilities in Adult Training Centres where they were often exploited as cheap labour doing packaging are now very much a thing of the past. The last Remploy Factory closed in 2012. However, clearly, they have not by 2025 been replaced by something meaningful. And reducing the benefits of people with disabilities to try to force some of the most disadvantaged people into employment will not provide meaningful work or encourage employers to take them on.

The advantage of the former "Sheltered Placement Scheme" was that the person with a physical disability or learning disability could be taken on and paid the same rate as other people doing the same job with any assessed loss in output, perhaps due to needing longer breaks or slower work etc, being made up and paid to the employer. This was so much better. And instead of cutting benefits, perhaps the Government could consider the reintroduction and development of this scheme. Most people on disability benefit would love to work for the right recognition and pay.

The development of Community Mental Handicap Teams (now Learning Disabilities) in the 1970s transformed the lives of many people with learning disabilities and their carers. With an emphasis on "normalisation" and the aid of the "sheltered placement scheme" the future looked bright. So how is it, that fifty years later, according to the Nuffield Trust only 4.8% of people with learning disabilities known to local authorities were in paid work in 2021 /22? People with learning disability can and do make hard working and enthusiastic employees. They bring new skills, talents and perspectives to their employers and, with the right support, they will remain loyal and longstanding employees.

Punishing people with disabilities or chronic illness for their misfortune by reducing their benefits in the mistaken belief that it will force them into work. is not the answer. Such conditions may, understandably, lead to depression and lack of motivation requiring professional intervention.

There is still a great deal of stigma attached to mental illness. And yet it is quite common with approximately 1 in 4 adults in the UK experiencing a mental health problem in any given year. And roughly 1 in 6 adults report experiencing a common mental health disorder, such as anxiety or depression, in any given week.

Mental health services have suffered from a lack of investment, been given low priority and the vital role of social work and social workers disregarded. In 2010/11, approximately 13.1% of the total NHS expenditure was allocated to mental health care including mental health problems amongst older people. According to Pulse Today the mental health budget is projected to be only 8.71% of the NHS baseline funding in 2025 /26. And yet the Covid 19 Pandemic was known to have taken a toll on mental health. The Charity MIND interviewed almost 12,000 people across England and Wales and:

- around a third of adults and young people said their mental health had got much worse since March 2020.
- 58% of people receiving benefits said their mental health was poor.
- 88% of young people said loneliness made their mental health worse during the pandemic.
- 1 in 5 adults did not seek support during the pandemic because they didn't think their problem was serious enough.

Hardly surprisingly therefore a significant proportion of individuals receiving disability benefits in the UK in 2024 had mental health problems. In fact, mental health conditions were the primary disabling condition for 44% of disability benefit claimants. And according to a study by the IFS 86% of incapacity and disability benefit claimants reported having a mental health condition, even if it was not their primary condition. They needed help, counselling and therapeutic intervention: not threats.

The 1959 Mental Health Act, with its emphasis on care in the community transformed the lives of many people. Particularly those who had spent 30 years or more in mental hospital sometimes for no other reason than having given birth to an illegitimate child. Social workers were key to the resettlement of such patients, with a growing understanding of the effects of institutionalisation, and the Act broadened the scope of services provided by local authorities. The 1959 Act established that entry to hospital for mental health treatment should be on medical, not legal, grounds and social workers approved under the 1959 Mental Health had a key part to play in this process. With the establishment of Social Service Departments in 1971 many Local Authorities confused the word "generic" (meaning common content) with "generalist" and authorised all its social workers regardless of qualification and experience under the 1959 Mental Health Act. Therefore the 1983 Mental Health Act built upon the 1959 Mental Health Act in requiring Social

Workers to undergo specific training before being authorised. It also strengthened the rights of people with mental health conditions, including introducing the concept of consent to treatment. During my time as an approved social worker under the 1959 Mental Health Act one of the most upsetting aspects was persuading a client to go to hospital as a voluntary patient only for them to be sectioned by a psychiatrist once in hospital – which, to me, was a betrayed of trust and would impede treatment. Fortunately this did not happen very often and rarely did I have to resort to a compulsory admission.

Since the turn of the century in 2000 social workers have become increasingly marginalised and the Mental Health Act 2007 diminished the role of social workers in compulsory admission by replacing the Approved Social Worker (ASW) role with the Approved Mental Health Professional (AMHP). This new role was open to a wider range of professions, including social workers, but it also meant that social workers were no longer the sole individuals responsible for making compulsory admission decisions.

Thus, the story is the same.

CHAPTER SIX - CARERS

Much of the consequence of the under-funding and disorganisation of the NHS and social care falls on carers. Many of whom were thrust into the role with very little notice or choice. According to the 2021 Census there were 5.8m unpaid carers in the UK of whom 1.7m provided more than 50 hours of unpaid care per week. The Centre for Care Research found that between 2010 and 2020 4.3m people became carers each year and, on average, 4m ceased to be carers each year. 59% of unpaid carers were women and 41% men. According to the 2021 Census it was women between 75 and 79 and men between 80 and 89 who were most likely to be giving in excess of 50 hours care each week.

The 2021 Census found that 3m carers of working age were in employment: and 2.7m not. Of those in work 38% were working part time compared with 29% of the none carer workforce. Carers UK found that 2.6m people had given up work to care – that was 600 per day. Therefore, there is also an impact on the economy with people unable to work due to caring responsibilities which were forced upon them in that they were left with very little alternative but to care for their loved ones.

Being thrust into caring can be a very stressful and traumatic experience and carers need practical and emotional support – which is often just not there. And if their loved one needs to go into a care home and is deemed a self-funder they are often waved away and told to find a care home with no prior experience or knowledge and all the emotional turmoil involved. And, in consequence, their loved one denied an independent verification of their wishes. Often going along with going into a care home to no longer be a burden on their family.

What a way to spend the last few years of ones' life.

Two other groups of particular concern are the parents of people with learning difficulties and parents with disabled children who wonder what will happen to their children when they are no longer around to care.

Research commissioned by Carers UK and conducted by WPI Economics found that 1.2 million unpaid carers lived in poverty, and 400,000 lived in deep poverty in the UK. Carers UK's most recent State of Caring 2024 survey found that 61% of unpaid carers were worried about living costs and managing in the future. And a quarter of carers (27%) were struggling to make ends meet and 28% of carers were cutting back on essentials like food and heating.

In extreme cases it was possible in 2025 to claim both Attendance Allowance of £110.40 per week, which is not means tested, and Carers Allowance of £83.30 per week. Making an annual income of £10,072.40p This compared with the living wage of £23,795 and Average Earnings of £38,224.

Centre for Care Research found that the economic value of the support provided by unpaid carers in England and Wales in 2025 was an estimated £162 billion per year, 29% more in real terms than 2011.

The 2021 Census in England and Wales found that about 1 in 4 carers reported 'not good health' after adjusting for age, compared with fewer than 1 in 5 non-carers. The 2024 GP Patient survey in the UK found that 70% of carers said they had a long-term physical or mental health condition, disability or illness. Research by Public Health England suggested that caring should be considered a social determinant of health. The most recent, at the time of writing, NHS SACE survey found that 20% of carers felt they were neglecting themselves. Carer's UK "State of Caring" survey 2023 found that over three quarters (79%) of carers felt stressed or anxious, and half of carers (49%) felt depressed. And 54% of carers said their physical health had suffered.

Clearly, providing more support to carers would be cost effective. But not all carers are of working age.

According to the 2021 Census there were approximately 120,000 young carers below the age of 17 years – some as young as 5 years of age in England and 8,200 in Wales. These are children who often have little choice but to care for their sick or disabled parent(s).

CHAPTER SEVEN
A MULTI-DISCIPLINARY
/ INTER-AGENCY APPROACH

As stated earlier very rarely can professionals in health and social care work in isolation and a multi-disciplinary approach is often required. Therefore, there is a need to remove functional divisions along patient / client pathways by the creation of multi-disciplinary, inter-agency, whole task, right-sized teams aligned behind outcome with access to all the resources required to achieve their goals. Communication is best within groups and worst between groups. Therefore, these teams need to operate out of a shared base at the focal point of the community of interest which they serve. This does not mean the dreaded open plan offices. (employers found during the pandemic that they got greater output from their employees who were home working free from the distraction and interruptions of open plan offices). These teams need to be able to "plan, do and evaluate" their own work which completes the "learning cycle" of "constant improvement" and enables them to gain the satisfaction derived from seeing the outcome of their interventions.

Social Workers need to be given the time and resources to do the job for which they were trained. A room to themselves in which to carry out diagnostic thought, write their reports and letters, make telephone calls and receive their clients in-order to make a differential use of office and home-based interviews is essential. The client should not be kept at arms-length in impersonal interview rooms but invited into the heart of the business into a room which reflects the personality of the social worker. A communal staff room where all involved might off load when returning from a stressful situation by just involving those there for similar reasons and not disrupting everyone else, also acts as a catalyst to team building and the mutual understanding of each other's role towards common shared goals.

All too often professionals are inadvertently working against each other.

There is so much which could be done to improve the effectiveness and efficiency of health and social care. A complete change of culture is required to liberate the dedicated, conscientious staff, who struggle to do a good job despite the system, rather than the organisation supporting them in their work – making it easier: not more difficult.

This requires structural, leadership and cultural change.

Since the 1990 National Health Service and Community Care Act the "contract culture" has led to:

    i. a "minding" rather than a "mending" service with social workers increasingly used to assess the eligibility to specific services, rather than using relationship, various therapeutic techniques and counselling to resolve problems;

    ii. providers being left with little discretion to respond in situ to changing need;

    iii. greater fragmentation with different components of a "package of care" bought from different providers, and;

    iv. "self-funders" (a dreadful term) being waived away denying them an "independent verification of their wishes" and their families the help and support they need.

The Griffiths Reforms also effected the NHS. The demise of Area Health Authorities and creation of Trusts with the internal market and purchaser / provider split added to the fragmentation and bureaucracy in the NHS. For example, during my time as a Non-Executive Director of an NHS Trust, all Trusts, or so we were told, had to have something called an "Integrated

Governance Committee". This turned out to be about "risk management" rather than "integrated governance". "The Integrated Governance Committee" consisting of twenty people, including the Chief Executive and Consultants, would spend up to two hours each month pouring over the risk register, which consisted almost entirely of equipment thought to be on its way out. The report then went to the Capital Prioritisation Committee. I do not know how long they spent on it but as they never had any capital to prioritise the report went virtually unchanged to the Audit Committee. The Audit Committee consisting of twelve people, including the Chief Executive and Consultants, spent another hour on virtually the same report saying how dreadful it all was. From there it went to the Management Team of the Trust and on to the Trust Board which spent another hour going through it. And then round it went again the next month. The only time anything was removed from the register was when it broke and had to be replaced. The cost of this in staff time amounted to a third of the cost of the risks involved suggesting that if it were not for the system all the risks could be removed in three months. To which the Director of Finance responded that it would be an "opportunity saving" as all the cost in staff salaries would remain. The Trust was making much needed ground staff redundant.

There I rest my case.

Income Inequality and Poverty – the impact on health and social care

CHAPTER EIGHT
POVERTY, HEALTH AND PENSIONS.

There is a wealth of empirical evidence on the "social determinates of health" (Marmet M et al, 2012) which has demonstrated the correlation between income and demand upon the NHS.

At just £9,152 (£11,804 with pension credit) Britain still had one of the lowest State Pensions in the western world in 2025. The national living wage was £25,397 and average earnings £37,800. The definition of poverty is less than 60% of median household income.

In 2021, approximately 3.3 million older people in England and Wales lived alone – representing 30.1% of the older population.

In 2024 there were two million older people living in poverty in Britain - many of whom, prior to the abolition of the "default retirement age" in 2012, were forced into retirement and condemned to spending the rest of their lives in poverty. There was no other group of people who could be treated in this way. Just imagine if people were denied employment on grounds of race, gender, religion or disability. And yet, until 2012 it was perfectly legal to deny employment on grounds of age. Research has shown that redundancy has a more long-term debilitating effect than either bereavement or divorce – forced retirement was like redundancy only more so as there was little hope of re-employment. There was little wonder, therefore, that there was so much depression amongst older people. And if they retired before April 2016 they were not entitled to the new State Pension either. The Government, in its wisdom, reduced the income of retired people further by first stopping the free television license and them suspending the "triple lock" for a year in 2023/24. The "triple lock", whereby the State Pension increases each year by whichever is the greater of prices, earnings or 2.5%, was introduced in 2010 to reverse the 30 years of erosion since the earnings link was removed. Prices are about the cost of living: earnings are about the standard of living and quality of life. As the economy grows so too do the expectations and necessities of life. For example, very few people had a fridge in the 1950s: it would be very difficult to live without one today. Between 2000 and 2010, when the "triple lock" was introduced, earnings went up by 41.7%, pensions linked to RPI increased by 32.4% and those linked to CPI a mere 26.6%. Low interest rates, for over a decade from 2010, meant that lifetime savings did not kept pace with inflation.

Banks need to have a re-think in respect of the interest they pay to savers (and charge on mortgages) taking into account their own high salaries, bonuses and profits.

And in 2024 the Government stopped the "winter fuel allowance" which had been part of older retired people's incomes since 1999. No other group of people had a pay cut. Stopping of the winter fuel allowance was compounded by the freezing of the personal tax-free allowance and income tax band thresholds by the previous government. Rather than raising these in line with inflation, which has been the traditional approach, in the run up to the 2024 General Election the Chancellor twice chose to cut National Insurance, in November 2023 and March 2024, which excluded those receiving their state pension from any benefit. Rising food and fuel prices, being essential items, hit the poor and older retired people disproportionately as these take up most of their income and, of course, in 2020 older people had also lost their free television licence.

It is hardly surprising given that Britain had, and in 2025 still had, one of the lowest State Pensions in the developed world that, before the COVID 19 pandemic killed 223,396 mainly older dependent people, 80% of the expenditure of the NHS was on older people. The Netherlands with the highest state pension in Europe spent 60% of its health budget on older people.

Income Inequality and Poverty – the impact on health and social care

Occupational Pensions were also eroded from 1971 onward, due in part to Gordon Brown's 1997 tax raid on pension funds, with "defined benefit" schemes being replaced by "defined contribution" ones" and many of the "defined benefit" schemes which survived going from "final salary" to "average salary". Since 1971 the index linking has gone from earnings to RPI to CPI – even for pensions in payment. And auto-enrolment into pension schemes did more to reduce the demand for "pension credit" than it did to increase income due to the small contributions made.

Older retired people singled out for a cut in income after the 2024 General Election.

After the 2024 General Election the incoming Labour Government made great play of the so called £22billion black hole as a reason for stopping the "winter fuel allowance" which, as stated earlier, had been part of older retired peoples' income since 1999.

The Office of Budget Responsibility estimated that the most recent 2% cut in National Insurance, in the run up to the General Election, would cost an average of £10.3billion per year over the following ten years. If one adds to that the previous 2% cut in National Insurance (a few months earlier) that would explain the £22billion short fall in public finances identified by the Government. Presumably, the previous Government hoped to recover this "give away" by growth and, more particularly, the frozen tax-free personal allowance which the Office of Budget Responsibility estimated would raise £35.7billion by 2028/29.

This being the case, it seemed most unfair and discriminatory for older retired people, who had no earning potential or borrowing power and got no benefit from the cuts in National Insurance but were affected by the frozen tax-free allowance, to be singled out as the only group of people to have a cut in income following the General Election. Doctors, nurses and train drivers had an immediate pay rise. Losing the winter fuel allowance was a £200 or £300 cut in both gross and net income for older retired people as it was not taxable.

Sometimes people have defended (the indefensible) by quoting the add ons such as the winter fuel allowance, free prescriptions and bus passes when comparing the British State Pension with that in other Countries. Older retired people recently lost their free TV licence and now their winter fuel allowance. Not only did this add to the hardship of older people, at the very time gas prices were set to increase (not of necessity but in search of profit born of greed) but given the correlation between

Income Inequality and Poverty – the impact on health and social care

income and demand upon the health services, would, and more than likely did, increase the winter pressures on the NHS at the very time the Government was committed to reducing waiting times.

The constant references to multi-millionaires getting the winter fuel allowance was a red herring and symbolic of other issues. It could be an expression of the widely felt anger at the widening income inequality and increasing poverty in the UK and worldwide. However, stopping the winter fuel allowance did not reduce income differentials but did widen income inequality and increase poverty. It was not in the Labour election manifesto and had exactly the opposite impact of the Government's declared intentions. Thankfully, it was restored for some the following year.

However, subsequently the Chancellor, Rachel Reeves, proposed merging Local Government Pension Schemes and consolidation with defined contribution pension schemes to create a mega-fund to unlock investment and boost growth. This was high risk and needed safeguards and guarantees. It was not Government or taxpayers' money but belonged to the members of each particular pension scheme and was in effect their retirement savings. When Gordon Brown altered the tax position of pension funds he sent many into deficit which brought about the demise of many defined benefit final salary schemes - with even the Local Government Schemes moving from "final salary" to "average salary". The index linking used to be to earnings, then RPI and more recently changed to CPI – even for pensions in payment.

These changes were not being proposed to improve pensions but to use pension funds to boost investment in search of growth. Economic growth was the Government's priority. But what were the risks and knock on effect of this proposal for pensioners?

When the Government re-instated the winter fuel allowance for 2025 / 26 there was no public recognition of the additional hardship it had caused older retired people or the additional winter pressure it had caused the NHS. It was done in response to the government's ranking in the opinion polls and loss of votes in the local elections. Nor did it do the obvious thing and add it to the state pension so that it became taxable.

And, as this second edition went to press Rachel Reeves proposed taxing unused defined contribution pensions. There are two assumptions underlying the government's apparent desire to reduce expenditure on, and take money from, older people. Firstly, that older people no longer contribute economically when many volunteers, trustees, carers and unpaid child minders are older retired people. And secondly that older people have a disproportionate share of wealth which is because older people have often paid off their mortgages during a lifetime of struggle but have very low incomes. Many of the older retired people in 2025 helped rebuild the country after the second world war and paid National Insurance with the promise of care "from cradle to grave". And yet in 2025 over two million of them were living in poverty many of whom, if they retired before the abolition of the "default retirement age" in 2012, had been forced into retirement and condemned to spending the rest of their lives in poverty.

As these pages have demonstrated to increase the state pension and raise the tax-free personal allowance to lift people out of poverty would improve the quality of life of all and save money. One cannot fix whole systems problems with component level solutions.

CHAPTER NINE – ECONOMIC GROWTH, INCOME INEQUALITY AND POVERTY

During her few days as Prime Minister in the UK, Liz Truss tried to boost the economy with £45b tax cuts, in her budget of the 23rd September 2022. This was putting into practice ideas she had developed in a paper she had co-written when at University. In her memoires she blame the Office of Budgetary Responsibility (OBR) and the Bank of England for obstructing her and causing the subsequent collapse. The Bank of England had publicly put aside £65b to cover Government Debt shaking the confidence in the market to invest.

But why should investors and stockbrokers hold such power. In the USA millions of pounds were knocked off the value of shares, and Tesla in particular, in April 2025: not because people had stopped buying Tesla cars but because the investors and stockbrokers thought they would, presumably because of Elon Musk's association with President Donald Trump and his trade tariffs. Part of the reason behind the tariffs, according to Donald Trump, being to encourage American Companies to manufacture in the US instead of outsourcing to cheap labour in China and other Countries. However, Tesla shares bounced back by an unheard of 23% and it was rumoured that Elon Musk made a few billion!!

It is questionable whether the Stock Market and Banks should have so much power over Governments and the economy? But this is the system under which the world economy operates in 2025 and one which must be brought into question.

There was widespread concern during the 2008 banking crisis that whilst the majority suffered austerity those the public were led to believe had brought about the crisis prospered. For example. as a result of the crisis the share value of the banks fell, but after the Government bailed them out share values rose and half the money paid to Royal Bank of Scotland, for example, went straight out in bonuses which were related to share values.

Between 2010 and 2020 the rich got richer and the majority poorer – ref the BBC 2 two-part series "The decade the rich won". "Trickle Down" economics and the privatisation of public services since the 1980's created dozens of millionaires and turned millionaires into billionaires whilst by 2025 the majority were no better off than they were before the 2008 Banking Crisis and millions had fallen into poverty.

Income Inequality and Poverty – the impact on health and social care

According to a report by the Paris-based World Inequality Lab, 2020 saw the steepest increase in billionaires' wealth on record, whilst the majority got poorer. Fifteen years of austerity in the UK since 2010 saw the rich prosper.

As a result of this widening income inequality there were, by 2024, 3.9 million children being brought up in poverty in the UK – 2/3rds of whom had a parent in work. These parents were no more able to increase their income than were older people who had no earning or borrowing capacity. Children brought up in poverty are less likely to do well at school, more likely to have health problems, making a demand upon the NHS, and have a shorter life expectancy.

According to Philip Alston, special rapporteur on extreme poverty to the UN, Government Ministers were in a "state of denial" about poverty. During a twelve day visit to the UK in 2019 he said that despite being in one of the world's richest countries he had encountered "misery". Quoting figures from the Joseph Rowntree Foundation, he said that more than 1.5 million people were destitute at some point in 2017, meaning they lived on less than £70 a week or went without essentials such as housing, food, clothing or heating. A fifth of the population, amounting to 14 million people, are living in poverty, Prof Alston said.

Income Inequality and Poverty – the impact on health and social care

In contrast the pay of Chief Executives at businesses on the FTSE 100 index surged 11% on a median basis during 2017 while average earnings failed to keep pace with inflation. And this trend continued with the 2024 cost of living crisis. According to Oxfam the wealth of global billionaires grew by £35m per day during 2024. Adding more weight to the fear that growth for billionaires is coming at the expense of the rest of the population and that the wealth was not being made by billionaires: it was being taken. Whilst reducing global poverty had been almost at a standstill since 1990 the wealth of those at the very top had skyrocketed. According to the Equality Trust the control this wealth gives billionaires over our societies had never been more visible. Polling from "Patriotic Millionaires", published in 2024, found that two-thirds of all millionaires thought that the super-rich were a threat to global stability, while 72% wanted higher taxes on the super-rich and 70% thought the super-rich were eroding trust in democracy by exerting control over the media. Widening income inequality and increasing poverty are the great social evils of our time. Unless Government tackles pay differentials chasing investment in pursuit of growth will favour the rich at the expense of working people, people with disabilities or illness, older retired people and children. It will make the rich richer and create low paid jobs for the masses as it has done since the 1980s – thereby widening income inequality.

The Apostle Paul said "the love of money is the root of all kinds of evil" by which he clearly meant GREED.

Perhaps it is time to legislate so that the lowest paid employee of any organisation is paid an agreed minimum percentage of the highest paid Director / Employee of that organisation (including the banks and utilities and Chief Executives and Chairmen) with the minimum wage as a back stop. Perhaps, bonuses should be based on an agreed percentage of profits (not related to share values or multiples of salaries) and shared pro-rata amongst all who contributed. Those at the top could still have their million-pound salaries provided they paid those on whose hard work they depend proportionately. Clearly this would not apply to people who earn on individual merit, from selling tickets, patents or royalties, but to those who depend upon the work of, and exploit, others often circulating around established companies creaming off millions for personal use. It would not be too dissimilar to Chief Officer grades in Local Government whereby a Deputy Chief Officer is paid 80% of the Chief Officer's salary and an Assistant Director 66% but would ripple down the whole organisation so that the lowest paid would also get a percentage of the highest paid – with the minimum wage as a back stop. It could be introduced over time with the equivalent of a "triple lock" whereby pay of all employees in an organisation went up by the same percentage as those at the top, by inflation or an amount agreed by the employer, which ever was the greatest until the agreed percentage was reached.

Individual Countries now operate in a global economy with the large corporations and multi-billionaires operating globally outside the control of individual Governments, fuelling income inequality and poverty worldwide. Governments need to come together to adapt to this changing world, possibly through the United Nations, to get to grips with this rapidly developing economic situation. At the time of writing France, Spain, South Africa and Brazil were trying to get international agreement to a minimum wealth tax on multi-billionaires to avoid them moving their money around countries. There is a positive and significant relationship between directors' pay and employees' average wage in Japan.

CHAPTER TEN - HOUSING

Food and shelter are essential to survival and yet according to the latest Government figures, collected in the autumn of 2019 and published in February 2020, 4,266 people were estimated to be sleeping rough each night in this the 5th largest economy in the world. The Charity Crisis believes it may be nearer to 8,000.

Until 1974 Homelessness was a social service responsibility but was transferred to housing on Local Government Reorganisation. This was responding to the "presenting problem" as very few people are born homeless and find themselves in that position due to a number of circumstances including eviction, debt, break down in relationships, mental health problems etc all of which require social work intervention. Clearly taking out the two-tier system so that housing and social services serve the same geographical areas with common funding streams and lines of accountability will help considerably here.

According to the charity Shelter three million new social homes must be built in England over the next 20 years of which 1.2 million homes are needed for younger families who cannot afford to buy and "face a lifetime in expensive and insecure private renting". The in-coming 2024 Labour Government committed to building 1.5 million new homes between 2024 and 2029, aiming for 370,000 homes annually with a focus on affordable houses, and relaxed planning restrictions to achieve this. Housing is big business where economic return appears to take priority over human need.

It was the collapse of the property marked in America which led to the economic crisis in 2008 which saw the Government bail out the banks and led to fourteen years of austerity during which the rich, including those responsible for the crisis, got richer and the majority got poorer.

In 2023 / 24 the Government got £11.61m from Stamp Duty paid on house purchase and the value of one's house is still taken into account in 2025 when assessing long term care charges – with an estimated 30,000 to 40,000 having to sell their houses to pay for their care each year. Despite the new allowance (introduced in April 2017) that allows couples to pass on a family home worth up to £850,000 tax-free, "Inheritance Tax" receipts hit a record high of £5.76bn in the 2020/21 tax year - much of it from houses.

Despite schemes like "Help to Buy" and the abolition of "stamp duty" for first time buyers many new so called "affordable homes" remained difficult to sell because there were too few would be first time buyers able to afford them. Building giants Barratts and Taylor Wimpey made pre-tax profits in 2019 (even after paying their Chief Executives £3.6m and £1.7m) of £909.8m and £656.8m respectively. Barratts built 17,856 houses thereby making a pre-tax profit (after all on costs) of £50,000 per house. The Nationwide Building Society made a pre-tax profit of £833m in 2019 after having paid its Chief Executive £2.37m, including bonuses, and this despite profits having fallen from an all-time high of £1.2bn in 2016.

Clearly there was sufficient money in the system to considerably reduce the price of new houses. House prices have to some extent been dictated by supply and demand and to reduce the price of new ones would have a knock-on effect on prices generally and leave many homeowners in negative equity – ie owing more on their houses than they are worth. Therefore, the answer lies, not in reducing prices (although this would clearly be possible) but in increasing the incomes of the lower paid including those in the building industry so that deposits and mortgages are within everyone's reach.

No matter what social problem one considers the cause usually comes down to inequality, social exclusion and poverty and therein must lie the solution.

We can't meet one basic human need by sacrificing another

Travelling around the UK in 2025 one got the impression that there was more house building going on than ever before with new estates springing up on green field sites gobbling up agricultural land. This was within 5 years of the UK leaving the EU and "single market" with the "common agriculture policy" and before the full impact was known. About 30% of all the UK's food was imported from EU Countries, particularly Spain, and for some products not grown here it was 100%. In 2016 more than £30.3bn of Britain's food imports and £12.3bn of its food exports were with the EU, totalling almost £1,300 of trade every second and highlighting the scale of the potential economic disruption. Therefore, there is an increasing demand for home produced food at a time agricultural land is being swallowed up.

Since the end of the Second World War and by 2025 there had been a 65% reduction in the number of farms in the UK and a 77% reduction in the number of people employed in agriculture. Remarkably productivity had increased fourfold.

In 2025 there were 23.07million acres of agricultural land in the UK although it was not possible to calculate how much land had been lost since the end of the Second World War in 1945. What is known is that the population of the UK was 48.67m in 1945 compared to 66.44m in 2025. During the Second World War, when it was difficult to get food from Europe, people were encouraged to have allotments to supplement vegetables produced by the then number of farms and which have declined since then,

Therefore, one must ask how many new homes do we actually need?

Statistics published by the Ministry of Housing, Communities and Local Government (MHCLG) put the number of empty homes in England in October 2018 at 634,453. This represented a 4.7% increase on the previous year's total. In 2019, there were 19.2 million families, an increase of 0.4% on the previous year, with a 6.8% increase over the decade from 2009 to 2019. The number of households grew by 0.9% since the previous year to 27.8 million in 2019, an increase of 6.8% over the previous 10 years.

Income Inequality and Poverty – the impact on health and social care

According to ONS figures there were 8.4 million people living alone in the UK in 2023 equating to 30% of all households and 13% of all people living in households. The ONS defines a household as one person living alone, a family, more than one family or no families in the case of a group of unrelated people.

In 2021, 3.3 million people aged 65 years and over were living alone in England and Wales, 30.1% of the older population. 36.3% of older women were living alone and 22.7% of older men. Older people who live alone are twice as likely to visit or be taken to A & E at hospital.

64,448 older people applied for equity release in 2023 to take money out of their houses to fund their retirement. This is a charge, plus interest, against their house when they die.

Addressing income inequality is key

Many of the 3.3 million older people who were living alone were in two, three and four bedroomed houses. Many would wish to stay in the home they know, where their memories are and where their children can visit. Others would down-size if suitable housing was available. The Government is intent on building family homes for first time buyers with very few bungalows. If more bungalows were built and the cost of moving – i.e

Income Inequality and Poverty – the impact on health and social care

stamp duty, estate agent fees, removal costs and legal fees etc – were not so great many older people might downsize – thus freeing up family homes.

Many of the 3.3 million older people who live alone are very lonely and rarely see anybody. More should be done to forge mutual friendships with information about "tenants in common" and "life interest trusts" to protect the inheritance of their respective children should older people wish to buy together. Two older people buying together as "tenants in common" with a "life interest trust" to enable the survivor to remain in the house on the death of the first until their death or the house is sold upon them entering permanent long-term care would only potentially spend the money they had each taken out of their respective houses. Unlike "equity release" where the interest builds up and is deducted from the equity in the house on death or sale, two people buying as "tenants in common" would be keeping the equity in their house intact for their heirs.

From the above it is clear that there is more than enough money in the system to considerably reduce the price of new houses so that they are affordable but this would have a knock-on effect and leave many homeowners in negative equity and is therefore not the solution. What is required is a redistribution of income so that houses are affordable for all and a rethink as to how need is met from within the existing housing stock.

With 634,453 empty houses and 8.4m single person households it should not be beyond the ingenuity of the human-race to meet the alleged shortfall of 1.2m homes without swallowing up more agricultural land. However, with so much money to be made out of the current system and house building it is doubtful that the needs of the wider population will be considered.

CHAPTER ELEVEN
SALARIES OF THE SUPER-RICH AND THE UTILITIES

The salaries of the superrich often run into millions as do their bonuses. It is thought that Bob Diamond, a former Chief Executive of Barclays, received in excess of his publicly declared £75m (possibly as much as £125m) over his five-year tenure whilst making 30,000 people redundant before moving on to pastures new leaving counter staff over worked and customers queuing for service. Many branches closed.

The "unacceptable face of capitalism" was evidenced again during the 2022 energy crisis. Gas was in short supply due to the war in Ukraine, but instead of the multi-national companies distributing pro-rata to previous demand they sold to the highest bidder adversely affecting the poorer countries and people on lower incomes in the richer ones whilst making excessive profits themselves.

The introduction of another tier in-order to take profit out of the system when the utilities were privatised in the 1980s by Margaret Thatcher made matters even worse in the UK. These energy companies were purely billing companies: they do not produce any gas or lay or repair any pipes. And yet in 2024 their Chief Executives were paid as follows: EON £1m, RWE £3.6m, Orsted £1.7m, Centrica £4.5m, SSE £1.6m, Uniper £1.6m, Scottish Power £1.15m, Drax £2.7m, EDF (which made a loss) £1m. How can these salaries be justified? Before privatisation there would have been one public sector Chief Executive for Gas and one for Electricity. The Chief Executive of Birmingham City Council was paid £186,000 in 2024 for arguably greater and certainly more complex responsibility.

It is difficult to believe that there are people worth so much more than people working in the public sector. It is often said that such high salaries are required to stop the talent going abroad. Could it be that the mind set of these individuals is wrong in focussing on profit above service? In which case let them go abroad there are many people here able to do just as good or better job for less money and do we really want a society motivated by greed? The aim of the public services should be to provide the best possible service at the least possible cost. The performance of the Water Companies leaves a lot to be desired, for example.

In 2024 the incoming Government announced its intention to re-nationalise the railways as contracts came up for renewal. Privatisation of the railways was ill-conceived as unlike a car, which can drive on any relatively smooth surface, a train is confined to the tracks. It is an integrated system and the train cannot be separated from the track. Therefore, the only way to privatise would have been region by region. But the whole rational behind privatisation is competition for customers. And this would not have applied on a regional basis any more than it did for the Water Boards. At the time of writing, in 2025, a YouGov survey found that 69% of respondents were in favour of the re-nationalisation of water.

And such high salaries may prove counter-productive in making the job that much harder and the organisation less, rather than more, productive. How must a low paid employee of the National Grid feel turning out at 2 am in the early hours braving horizontal rain to climb a ladder to restore electricity knowing his Chief Executive is most likely warm and dry with his £6.5m salary in the bank. To quote Charles Handy from the "Age of Unreason" (Handy, 1989) "The leader must remember that it is the work of others. The vision remains a dream without the work of others". What must these high salaries and wage differentials do for motivation, output and morale.

Between them these "billing companies" made over £30billion in profit during 2022.

If one added the excess profits of the produces to those of the retailers (billing companies) and allowing for commercial consumption it would have gone a long way towards avoiding crippling price increases for the 28.2 million households in the UK. However, unlike much of Europe, the British Government chose to borrow money to help households, which will have to be paid back through income tax, rather than imposing a windfall tax – or taking the retail utility companies back into public ownership.

And given that most of the UK's electricity was, by 2025, generated in house it is hard to see why these prices also soared. There was no logic behind linking gas and electricity prices.

According to several public opinion surveys held between 2022 and 2024 the public would favour the utilities (retail), NHS, social services and education being not for profit or in public ownership.

To abolish the "standing charge" on electricity and gas bills and spread it across the unit costs would benefit those who use smaller amounts of gas and electricity.
Cold homes increase the risk of respiratory and cardiovascular diseases, leading to a surge in deaths during winter. Respiratory illnesses like pneumonia and chronic obstruction pulmonary disease are significantly

more prevalent in winter, contributing to a large portion of excess winter deaths. Cold weather can put a strain on the cardiovascular system, increasing the risk of heart attacks and strokes. The World Health Organisation estimates that cold homes contribute to 30% of all excess winter deaths. The Office of National Statistics calculates that there were 13,400 excess winter deaths in England and Wales during the winter of 2021 / 22.

CHAPTER TWELVE
INCOME INEQUALITY, POVERTY, HEALTH AND SOCIAL CARE: A WHOLE-SYSTEMS APPROACH?

Earlier chapters have considered the organisation of health and social services and the need for radical reform, restructuring and cultural change; in-order to liberate the dedicated staff from the constraining contract culture into an enabling leadership one. And the wealth of evidence around the social determinates of health which has demonstrated the corelation between income and demand on health and social care.

An estimated 1.3million older people in the UK suffer from malnutrition costing the NHS £22.6billion per year. There are five main contributary factors to malnutrition: lack of money; lack of motivation; incapacity; lack of support and social isolation.

How can one of the richest Countries in the world allow its older citizens to virtually starve to death or die from hyperthermia during the winter in twenty-first century, Britain? And allow 29% of its children to be brought up in poverty?

All the figures in this chapter are at a 2025 price base. So, what might the outcome have been had

Income Inequality and Poverty – the impact on health and social care

the Government chosen to use its estimated savings on Local Government Reform (£2.9b) and the abolition of NHS England £100m) to pump prime the ripple effect of the radical reform of health and social care based upon a "whole systems review" by:

a.   bringing all services together, reinstating and reconfiguring Area Health Authorities and Police Authorities as Statutory Committees of the proposed Unitary Authorities in-order to achieve shared geographical areas, common funding streams and common lines of accountability: returning health and police to local democratic scrutiny within central government direction and taking out a tier of local government, making collaboration easier and saving a minimum of £4b on the cost of democracy and senior management.

b.   removing the purchaser / provider split and specialist commissioning, replacing it with a statutory, voluntary, private sector partnership.

c.   Freeing up social workers to practice their skills in using relationship and various therapeutic techniques to resolve problems and reduce the demand for state funded long term care.

d.   making other requisite organisational, leadership and cultural change to:

i.   liberate professionals and organisations working directly with people from the "straight jacket" of the "contract culture" enabling them to respond in situ to changing need, innovate and develop (the "contract culture" has meant that the private and voluntary sectors have been micro- managed – the voluntary sector was renowned for innovation and development which the statutory sector was only too pleased to grant aid);

ii.   remove functional divisions along patient / client pathways by the creation of "whole task, right sized, multidisciplinary, inter-agency teams", co-ordinated by the most senior employee from the lead agency in each team, with "key workers" at case level – these teams should be aligned behind outcome and able to "plan, do and evaluate" their own work which completes the learning cycle of constant improvement and have access to all the resources they need to achieve the desired outcome;

iii.   these teams to operate out of a "shared base" as communication is best within groups and worst between groups – this does not mean in "open-plan" offices as professionals need a room to themselves for diagnostic thought, face time and telephone calls, report writing and in-order to make a differential use of home and office-based contact – a shared staff room to enable catharsis after stressful contact and facilitate team building;

iv.   move from a "prescribing management culture" to an "enabling leadership culture" recognising that staff are working in their chosen vocation and the role of management to paint the vision, give strategic direction, manage the external environment, train and enable, monitor and evaluate, and;

v.   agree a strategy with the Trades Unions to end the use of agency staff to save money and ensure greater continuity of care with the savings shared in higher salaries for all.

any savings from these changes be used to improve the quality and quantity of services and improve salaries.

e.   work with Housing Associations and the Private Sector to develop extra-care sheltered housing with nomination rights and a base for the "multi-disciplinary teams" working with older people in the locality providing outreach on a "core and cluster" basis.

f.   encourage the building of bungalows and look at ways of providing financial incentives for older retired people to downsize should they so choose;

g.   look at ways of combating social isolation amongst older people and at ways of making a better use of existing housing stock by "tenants in common" and "life interest trusts";

h.   ensure that all older people have a "verification of wishes", help in considering the alternatives before being admitted to a "care home" and their carers the support they need;

i.   raising the State Pension to 60% of average earnings to lift all older people out of poverty (3.8m older people live alone) or £22,934, which would still be lower than much of

Europe and less than the "living wage" of £25,397 (at a cost of £132b). This would absorb pension credit (£5b - which only had a 63% take-up), housing benefit and council tax relief (£20b);

j.   extend NI to all working people, including those entitled to their state pension who have continued to work, (£3.9b) with the State Pension only paid on retirement with phased arrangements – ie one day's work – 4/5th pension (saving an additional £8.04b);

k.   this increased State Pension would currently be above the free personal tax-free allowance and thereby taxable with a minimum of 20% clawed back from people with other income through taxation (£22b). Therefore, the NET cost of increasing the state pension to 60% of average earnings to lift all older people out of poverty would be £73.06b after the changes in NI and pension entitlement. The cost is considerably more than when previously looked at prior to the pandemic which should not have been the case given the "triple lock". However, the "triple lock" was suspended for the 2022/23 financial year as it was thought the published increase of 8% in average earnings was a blip due to people going back to work after the pandemic – clearly not. Instead of going up by 8% the state pension increased by 3.1% in line with CPI (Consumer Prices Index) instead of the triple lock formula. And this is why, yet again, older retired people have fallen behind the working population;

l. free prescriptions and bus passes (which encourage older people to get out and are effectively a subsidy on less profitable routes combating global warming) would continue;

m. reconfiguring housing benefit. Currently someone on pension credit gets their rent paid whereas an owner occupier on pension credit doesn't get anything towards repairs or maintenance. The wide variation in rents, from the medium rent of £495 per month in the North-East to £1,425 per month in London makes it impossible to totally absorb housing benefit in the increased pension. Therefore, it is necessary to retain a limited means tested housing benefit so that no individual has to pay more than £250 per month rent, or mortgage interest, (£500 a couple) out of their new increased State Pension, at a cost of £5b;

n.   consider ways of increasing the tax-free personal allowance to 60% of medium household income so that no one in poverty pays tax and raising the income tax thresholds by a redistribution of the tax burden so the higher earners pay more to make it cost neutral;

o.   re-examine the wisdom behind the privatisation of the gas and electricity companies and of the water boards;

p.   consider removing the "standard charge" from gas and electricity bills and spreading it across the unit cost with, perhaps, the unit cost increasing the more gas and electricity one uses.

q.   enter into international discussion, through the United Nations, about tackling income inequality and poverty with a view to regulating pay differentials, particularly in the major corporations, by linking the salaries of all employees to the pay of those at the top.

The reform of Health and Social Care, better use of the existing housing stock, increasing the state pension and tax-free personal allowance is within the gift of the UK Government. Although this would marginally reduce income inequality and poverty to make real in roads would require a concerted international effort. As widening income inequality and increasing poverty is a global issue requiring a global response.

Clearly, the changes which are within the gift of the UK Government would enhance the lives of so many people and of those working in health and social care but what might the financial payback be?

To reduce malnutrition amongst older people by 90% would save £20.34billion. And given the correlation between income and demand upon the NHS there could be a further reduction in demand of between 10% and 15% or £18.36b as a result of lifting all older people out of poverty. The abolition of NHS England, creation of unitary authorities and amalgamation of the NHS and police could save another £4b. Therefore, the long-term net cost of these proposals would be £38.7b. The Government has committed an additional £25.6b to health and social care from 2026 onward. Therefore, the Government would have another £13.7b to find.

There would be additional savings on not having to means test pension credit and the freeing of hospital beds. Although some of this might have to be transferred to increase the provision of social care.

Given these changes and the higher State Pension there would no longer be a need to take capital into account when charging for care. And if people no longer had to sell their house to pay for their care it would increase Government revenue through inheritance tax thereby providing further income to offset against the cost.

In 2025 there were 278,946 older people in care homes in England and Wales (down from 416,000 in 2021), many of whom would be "self-funders", and it is anticipated that the number might decrease by up to 20%, as a result of this radical reform based upon a "whole systems approach", to 223,156.

Some research by Joyce McDonald in the 1970s which regularly monitored the deterioration of a group of older people against a number of indicators in order to identify matched pairs where one went into residential care (care home) and one didn't found that the one that went into the care home improved quite dramatically during the first six to eight weeks after which they began to deteriorate more rapidly than before with a shorter life expectancy than the one that did not go in – in every case. This suggests that residential care should, where-ever possible, be used for short stay respite care. (but not for people with Alzheimer's Disease or dementia who should be looked after in the familiar surroundings of their own home or one move into a care home as short stay respite care can disorientate them and make their subsequent care more demanding).

Extra-care Sheltered Housing can alleviate many of the harmful effects of institutionalisation. One can put just as much nursing and personal care into extra care housing developments as the more traditional residential care but the person has their own front door, defended space and retains control over the essentials of daily living. And, of course, their house cannot be taken into account in any financial assessment because they are living in it. The relationship between the resident and staff is also very different reducing the risk of abuse.

When Bob Bessell, the former Director of Social Services in Reading and Warwickshire, formed "Retirement Security Ltd" he took into account the income from Estate Agents fees on the resale of the flats in the financial projections in his business plan. However, the people who bought his flats lived much longer than initially expected throwing the financial projections out. Clearly, extra care housing is a preferred option.

Income Inequality and Poverty – the impact on health and social care

There will, however, continue to be a limited need for the more tradition care homes and nursing homes.

The average cost of a care home in 2025 was £49,348 per year. (up from £35,000 in 2020 - nursing care is already paid for) People would hand over their income up to the cost of the home, less their personal allowance of £30.65p per week, as now per CRAG.

With an increased pension of £22,934 the minimum residents could contribute would be £21,953 leaving a maximum of £27,398 (up from £18,117 when this calculation was first done in 2021) for the local authority to find. (Under CRAG people are deemed to have £1 per week income for every £250 of capital they have, including their house, between the disregard and full cost thresholds and this would no longer apply).

Some people with occupational or private pensions might, with this increased State Pension, be able to pay the full cost whilst still retaining their personal allowance. It did not prove possible to find out exactly how many people had other income or how much it was. The only reliable figure was the 1.5m people claiming pension credit which, given the poor take up, was 63% of those who would require the full £27,398. The best estimate (based on retirement income surveys) to totally disregard capital (including one's house), given this increased pension, would be an additional £3.5b – the Government estimated its cap at £86,000 would have cost £5.4b. Although the cost of care homes has sky rocketed since 2021 the number of care homes and older people in them has declined, partly due to the COVID 19 pandemic.

The total cost of these proposals is therefore £76.56b and the eventual savings £44.7b (plus that redeployed from organisation changes to increase output and effectiveness) giving a long-term cost of £31.86b. The Government has committed an additional £25.6b to health and social care from 2026 onward.

Therefore, the Government would only have to find an additional £6.26b to transform the lives of so many.

Regrettably, had Government chosen to use the £57.5b it threw at the failed 2021 Health and Social Care Act differently, and increased the state pension then, it would have had money back to reduce the tax burden on working people. Which was the situation the first time this was looked at in 2021.

What has widened the gap in respect of increasing the State Pension to lift all older retired people out of poverty since it was looked at it previously in 2020 was the suspension of the "triple lock" in 2022 /23 when had the triple lock been applied the State Pension would have gone up by 8% but was only increased by 3.1%. In 2020 the State Pension (£7,430) was 24.5% of average earnings (£30,212). By 2025 the State Pension (£8,814) had dropped to 23% of average earnings (£38,224). Added to which the stopping of the "winter fuel allowance", which represented a further cut of 3% in the income associated with the universal state pension, and which in the earlier calculations was to have been absorbed into the increased state pension off setting some of the cost and would, of course, have become taxable. And older people got no benefit from the two pre- election cuts in National Insurance.

More of the same only more so does not always work and sometimes the opposite is required to achieve the desired outcome. Concerns about the cost of an ageing population have led to raising the age of entitlement to the state pension and stopping the free TV licence and winter fuel allowance. When what might have been required, given the wealth of empirical evidence into the social determinates of health which has demonstrated the correlation between income and demand upon the health services, was an increased state pension to lift older people out of poverty and reduce demand upon the NHS and social care. If older people did need continuing long-term care (using the same financial assessment which has been in place since 1948 under CRAG) they would be able to pay more reducing the cost to the local authority and removing the need to take capital and one's house into account in the financial assessment. And, ultimately save money.

Widening income inequality and rising poverty are at the root of so many of the problems of the 21st century.

There were 4.5million children being brought up in poverty in the UK in April 2024 – 100,000 more than the previous year. 70% of whom had a parent in work. Clearly, the minimum wage is no longer fit for purpose and more needs to be done to address wage differentials within organisations. To quote Charles Handy from the Age of Unreason: "The leader must remember that it is the work of others. The vision remains a dream without the work of others".

Shortly after taking office in 2024 the Prime Minister stated there would be no more money for the NHS without reform. And yet the ten-year plan published in the summer of 2025 appears to be just accelerating the direction of travel. When what was needed was radical reform, restructuring and cultural change to liberate the dedicated professionals from the controlling contract culture into a more enabling leadership one. Social Work was grossly undervalued and social workers misused. Social work offers a great opportunity to resolve problems before long term state care is required.

The challenge is to get, and keep, people talking about the causes of income inequality and poverty and the possible solutions so that they become familiar, thereby acceptable and begin to gain traction. Most of the recommendations within this book are within the gift of Government. It will take "Political Will" driven by "popular demand" to bring about change.

Perhaps Government could do an income inequality and poverty audit on all it does to ensure that it is reducing income inequality and poverty and not increasing them?

References

Bainton D (23rd March1995) Building Blocks – Health Service Journal

Billis D and Rowbothan R (1985) The Stratification of Work and Organisation Design – Occasional Papers – Brunel University.

Griffiths R (1988) Community Care: An Agenda for Action – HMSO

Handy C (1989) The Age of Unreason – Business Books Ltd

Hollis F (1964) Casework: A Psychosocial Therapy – Random House NY

Marmet M et al (2012) – European review of social determinates of health and the health divide. – The Lancet

Peters T (1992) Liberation Management – Alfred A Knopf

Seebohm F (1968) The Report of the Committee on Local Authority and Allied Personal Social Services - HMSO

Income Inequality and Poverty – the impact on health and social care

ABOUT THE AUTHOR

Now retired, Chris J Perry MA CSW is a former Director of Social Services for South Glamorgan County Council, a former Non-Executive Director of the Winchester and Eastleigh Healthcare NHS Trust, a former Director of Age Concern Hampshire and a former presenter of an award-winning current affairs programme on Express FM.

His 34 years in Local Government / Social Services included twenty years as a deputy or chief officer and eight years as the Director of Social Services for South Glamorgan County Council. It embraced County Boroughs, Metropolitan Boroughs and County Councils in the north and south and England and Wales. And included both Conservative and Labour controlled Councils.

Early Life

Born in Yorkshire he was granted special dispensation to be warranted as a Cub Master at the age of 16 years, and during his late teens and early twenties promoted dances / concerts at three venues and managed rock groups which played at venues from Cleethorpes Pier

Income Inequality and Poverty – the impact on health and social care

in the East to the Floral Hall in Morecombe to the West and from Leeds to the north to Newark to the south. During this time he raised a considerable sum of money for the Scout Group and Community Association, of which he was a Committee Member, enabling the building of a Community Hall in the village in which he grew up.

He represented his school at Chess and Table Tennis. Won school prizes for "general excellency" at "O" level and the prize (only one per year) for "outstanding services to the school" in the upper sixth form.

Having passed his driving test at 17 years 3 months he sold ice cream in the summer and delivered Esso Blue in the winter to gain driving experience and earn money.

SHEFFIELD COUNTY BOROUGH COUNCIL.
10 years 4 months.

Welfare Assistant Trainee
Jan 61 – June 1964 – 3 years 6 months

Worked on the Sheffield Gale Relief Fund Seconded Social Work Training

Social Welfare Officer
June 1964 – May 1967 – 3 years

Area Social Welfare Officer
May 67 – Apr 71 – 4 years

Area Social Services Officer
READING COUNTY BOROUGH COUNCIL.
April 1971 – April 1975 – 4 year 1 month

Member of the management team of a new Social Services Department bringing together the former Children's Department, Welfare Department, Mental Health Department and Hospital Social Work Departments.

Seconded Masters' Degree in Public and Social Administration at Brunel University.

Assistant Divisional Director of Social Services – BERKSHIRE COUNTY COUNCIL.
Apr 1974 – July 1975 – 1 year 4 months

Deputy Director of Social Services
BOLTON METROPOLITAN BOROUGH COUNCIL
July 1975 – Dec 1982 – 7 years 6 months

Known for the Bolton Child Care Package. See "The Shocking Case of a Successful Department" (Social Work Today 19/5/81) and "Nothing Succeeds Like Success" (Community Care 1-10-81). During his time as Deputy Director of Social Services for Bolton Metropolitan Borough Council, between 1975 and 1982, the number of children in care was reduced from 660 to 487 and those in residential care from 286 to 107. The number of children placed out-county in high-cost CH(E)s was reduced to none and there was a significant reduction in the number of offences associated with juveniles. Bolton was amongst the pioneers for Contractual (paid) Foster Parents and of Very (or extra care) Sheltered Housing Schemes" . An inter-agency approach enabled more older people to remain in their own homes. Of 122 people who prior to 1982 would have entered residential care during an emergency and remained there only 33 were admitted of whom 21 later returned home. .

Bolton was the test site for SOSCIS the ICL Social Services Computer Based Client Record and Statistical System and Chris demonstrated the package to numerous Local Authorities

Income Inequality and Poverty – the impact on health and social care

SOUTH GLAMORGAN COUNTY COUNCIL
Jan 1982 – June 1995 – 12 years 6 month

Deputy Director of Social Services
Jan 1983 – Oct 1987 – 4 years 10 months

Recruited as Deputy Director in 1983 to articulate a complete set of client group related policies, develop strategies for their implementation and decentralise the department. After his restructuring, South Glamorgan had fewer tiers of management and more staff in direct client contact than any other Social Services Department. Services were delivered via inter-agency teams based in a network of Family Centres (the most recent of which were integral to schools), Resource Centres for people with a physical disability, Resource Centres for people with learning disabilities, Community Mental Health Centres, Community EMI Teams and Resource Centres for Older People. There were also social workers in hospitals and primary care and an integrated youth justice system.

Chris' experience as Deputy Director of Social Services for Bolton Metropolitan Borough Council, which had been the test site for SOSCIS (the ICL Social Services Package), enabled the in-house development of a comprehensive computer-based record and information system in South Glamorgan. Chris had his photograph on the front cover of "ICL at Work".

Seconded on a Senior Management Development Course run by the Local Government Training Board and National Institute for Social Work – one day per month.

Director of Social Services
Oct 1987 – June 1995 – 7 yrs 9 months

Chris headed a department with 3000 employees. Financial controls were praised by the Charter Mark Assessors with an out-turn within 0.1% of Cash Limit in each of the last six years for which he was Director.

• Between 1983 and 1995 the number of children in care (legal status – including those "looked after" and home "charge and control") was reduced from 986 to 274 and those in residential care from 386 to 87.
• South Glamorgan hosted NIMROD which was to the vanguard of the All Wales Mental Handicap Strategy and forerunner of the community care reforms.
• By 1995 South Glamorgan had the lowest number of older people in residential care as a percentage of the total population of any authority in Wales and the 6th lowest in Great Britain (he subsequently discovered that Wales counted "self-funders" where as England did

not). The number of residential homes directly managed by the County Council was reduced from 27 to 7.
• Only Gwynedd, out of all Social Services Departments in England and Wales supported more people with a physical disability in their own home.
• A life time campaigner for the reform of the Criminal Justice System - Chris was a strong advocate, and successful implementer, of policies of diversion and alternatives to custody - working tirelessly to reduce delay and put together programmes which interested and fully occupied young people throughout their waking hours. As a consequence reported crime went up less steeply in South Glamorgan, than the National Average, and fell on five occasions. The number of offences associated with juveniles fell by 34.3% between 1983 and 1993 and by a further 8% in 1994. In 1983 there were 94 children placed out-County in high cost Community Homes with Education on the premises: by 1995 there had been none for several years.

The department won many awards and accolades including:
i) The Play Wales Cup (1993) – for involving users and providers in the Sec 19 Review;
ii) Joint Investigation of Child Abuse highlighted as best practice by Oxford University and Channel Four following The Cleveland Enquiry;

iii) South Glamorgan had the most comprehensive Youth Justice System – NACRO (1993)

iv) 7 of the 22 examples of alternatives to secure accommodation in a Social Information Systems survey were drawn from South Glamorgan;

v) Strategy for Children with Challenging Behaviour included as best practice by the Audit Commission in "Seen But Not Heard" (1994);

vi) "Leaving Care Strategy" featured best practice in collaboration between social services and housing by CHAR (1994)

vii) Adolescent Complex – Care Home of the Year Award (1990)

viii) Gabalfa Workshop – first prize Community Care awards (1989)

ix) Rumney Computer Workshop – runner up (1990)

x) Delegations from Germany, Spain and Japan to look at NIMROD

xi) New Technology award (1995)

xii) Won two and came second in a third of five categories in respect of the implementation of the 1990 National Health and Community Care Act

In 1989 Chris attended the first European Skunk Camp as a guest of the Tom Peters Group and reached an agreement whereby one member of his management team went each year.

Chris took early retirement due to local government reorganisation in Wales and the abolition of the County Councils in 1995.

Consultant Trainer
June 1995 – August 1997 – 2 years 3 months

Associate Consultant – Work Structuring Ltd, BASE, Family Support Network at the University of East Anglia.

Evaluated the pilot EPICS (Elderly Persons Integrated Care System) projects, based on On Lok and PACE in the USA on behalf of the Helen Hamlin Foundation and ran seminars for Chief Executives and Directors from Health, Social Services and Housing.

Ran Seminars, with Christian Schumacher (the son of the author of "Small Is Beautiful), for Chief Executives and Directors from Health, Social Services and Housing, residential courses for Management Consultants on Christian's unique "whole systems methodology" and participated in consultancy.

Director Age Concern Hampshire
Aug 1997 – Aug 2012 – 15 years 1 month

In 1997 Age Concern Hampshire had a turnover of £604,578 and employed 81 people: in 2012 it had a turn-over of £2.7m and employed 181 people with a further 452 people who regularly gave of their services in a voluntary capacity.

The Worthy Of Work and pensions campaign launched in 1998 highlighted 38 people who had experienced age discrimination on television, radio and in the press. Chris was awarded an individual "Age Positive Champion" in 2004 in recognition of his campaigning against age discrimination in the workplace.

Consequent upon the legal challenge to the "default" retirement age of 65, contained in the Employment Equality (Age) Regulations 2006, Chris represented 26 people at Employment Tribunal whose cases were "stayed" pending the recommendation of the European Court. Anna John's whose case was initially "struck out" made legal history when she firstly won on appeal and then had that decision upheld in the Royal Courts of Justice resulting in a directive to all Employment Tribunals.

Chris had a petition on the Number 10 Website, during

the passage of the Equality Bill through Parliament and in the run up to the General Election in 2010, calling upon the Prime Minister to "end discrimination against, and poverty amongst, older people" which reached number 8 out of 293 in the economics and finance section and 154 out of 4,665 petitions over all. The incoming Government abolished the default retirement age and restored the earnings link.

During his last year, despite the recession, he was able to increase the turn-over, increase the number of people employed, obtain "Investors In People GOLD", retain ISO9001 and the quality standard for "Information and Advice" whilst turning in a surplus.

None- Executive Director – Winchester and Eastleigh Healthcare NHS Trust
Aug 2004 – March 2007 – 2 years 7 months

Radio Presenter – Express FM
March 2007 – Sept 2020 – 13 years 7 months

During his time with Age Concern Hampshire Chris edited it's newspaper, "there's more to LIFE" which peaked at a 35,000 circulation and from March 2007 presented a weekly radio programme on Express FM, choosing and researching his topics, writing the script, selecting and interviewing his guests (which included

Income Inequality and Poverty – the impact on health and social care

Cabinet Ministers, Chairman, Chief Executives, Academics, people with a story to tell and Celebrities), choosing the music, researching the artists presenting and recording the show with ongoing campaigns initially coinciding with those of Age Concern Hampshire. He continued with the programme in his own name when leaving Age Concern Hampshire.

Chris won the award for "Best Specialist Speech Based Programme" in 2008 and again in 2011.

Proprietor Twin Oaks Guest House
July 2007 – Dec 2019 – 12 years 6 months.

Chris and Carol (this was mainly down to Carol) built upon their individual achievements with their Four Star, Silver Accolade Guest House, with a Visit Britain Breakfast Award, and got excellent reviews on "TripAdvisor" winning the TripAdvisor Excellence Award in 2013, 2014, 2015, 2016, 2017, 2018 and again in 2019 with an entry in the TripAdvisor "Hall of Fame". Twin Oaks had a grade five food hygiene rating and "Good Hotel Guide" and "Les Routier" listings. In addition to Bed and Breakfast Chris and Carol ran "Photography Workshops" and a Cruise Service whereby people stayed the night before their cruise, left their car and transport was arranged to and from the cruise terminal.

Income Inequality and Poverty – the impact on health and social care

Membership of Professional Associations

As convenor of the Sheffield SCOSW group in the 1960s, he was an original member of BASW (644) and served on Council, as Vice Chair of the Professional Practice Divisional Committee and a Branch Chair. He was granted Honorary Membership of BASW (The British Association of Social Workers) at the 2012 AGM.

The lead Director in Wales for children's services and youth justice he was Vice Chair of Children in Wales and a Lord Chancellors appointment to the Area Criminal Justice Liaison Committee for South Wales.

A member of the Association of Directors of Social Services, Children and Families Committee he was the spokesperson on Youth Justice.

He was an advisor to the Association of County Councils. A member of the Young Offenders Committee of NACRO and on the committee of the National Children's Bureau. And a member of Advisory Group of The Audit Commission – on the well being of children – "Seen But Not Heard" – subsequently doing work on "Troublesome Youth"

He was Chair of the Cowbridge Citizen' Advice Bureau and of the Vale Money Advice Bureau. And Vice President of South Wales Relate.

In 2004 he was awarded an "Age Positive Champion" in recognition of his campaigning against age discrimination in the workplace.

Personal Life

Chris has two children, Ian and Donna, by his first wife Josie. And two granddaughters, Emily and Katie.

He has three stepsons, Stuart, Richard and James, by his second wife, Carol. And three step grandchildren, Layna, William and Oliver.

Printed in Dunstable, United Kingdom